OUR
SOUTHERN NEIGHBOR
MEXICO

THE GOVERNMENT OF MEXICO

CLARISSA AYKROYD

This political banner in Mexico City shows Zapatista terrorists and communist symbols. Throughout its history, Mexico has had to contend with a great deal of political instability. Numerous corrupt or ineffective governments have collapsed or been overthrown, particularly in the past century.

OUR
SOUTHERN NEIGHBOR
MEXICO

THE GOVERNMENT OF MEXICO

CLARISSA AYKROYD

Mason Crest Publishers
Philadelphia

Mason Crest Publishers
370 Reed Road
Broomall PA 19008
www.masoncrest.com

First printing

1 3 5 7 9 8 6 4 2

Library of Congress Cataloging-in-Publication Data

Aykroyd, Clarissa.
The Government of Mexico / by Clarissa Aykroyd.
    p.   cm. — (Mexico: our southern neighbor)
Includes bibliographical references and index.
Summary: Examines the history of government in Mexico,
discussing native and Spanish governments up to the nineteenth
century, independence, wars and reforms, and the Constitution
of 1917.
ISBN 1-59084-090-9 (hc)
1. Mexico—Politics and government—Juvenile literature.
[1. Mexico—Politics and government.] I. Title. II. Series.
F1226.A97 2002
972—dc21
                                   2001051421

TABLE OF CONTENTS

OUR SOUTHERN NEIGHBOR MEXICO

Roger E. Hernández
Senior Consulting Editor

INTRODUCTION

exico is a country in the midst of great change. And what happens in Mexico will have an important impact on the United States, its neighbor to the north.

These changes are being put in place by President Vicente Fox, who was elected in 2000. For the previous 71 years, power had been held by presidents from one single party, known in Spanish as *Partido Revolucionario Institucional* (Institutional Revolutionary Party, or PRI). Some of those presidents have been accused of corruption. President Fox, from a different party called *Partido de Acción Nacional* (National Action Party, or PAN), says he wants to eliminate that corruption. He also wants to have a friendlier relationship with the United States, and for American businesses to increase trade with Mexico. That will create more jobs, he says, and decrease poverty—which in turn will mean fewer Mexicans will find themselves forced to emigrate in search of a better life.

But it would be wrong to think of Mexico as nothing more than a poor country. Mexico has given the world some of its greatest artists and writers. Carlos Fuentes is considered one of the greatest living novelists, and poet-essayist Octavio Paz was awarded the Nobel Prize for Literature in 1990, the most prestigious honor a writer can win. Painters such as Diego Rivera and José Clemente Orozco specialized in murals, huge paintings done on walls that tell of the history of the nation. Another famous Mexican painter, Rufino Tamayo, blended the "cubist" style of modern European painters like Picasso with native folk themes.

Tamayo's paintings in many ways symbolize what Mexico is: A blend of the culture of Europe (more specifically, its Spanish version) and the indigenous cultures that predated the arrival of Columbus.

Those cultures were thriving even 3,000 years ago, when the Olmec people built imposing monuments that survive to this day in what are now the states of Tabasco and Veracruz. Later and further to the south in the Yucatán Peninsula, the Maya civilization flourished. They constructed cities in the midst of the jungle, complete with huge temples, courts in which ball games were played, and highly accurate calendars intricately carved in stone pillars. For some mysterious reason, the Mayans abandoned most of these great centers 1,100 years ago.

The Toltecs, in central Mexico, were the next major civilization. They were followed by the Aztecs. It was the Aztecs who built the city of Tenochitlán in the middle of a lake in what is now Mexico City, with long causeways connecting it to the mainland. By the early 1500s it was one of the largest cities anywhere, with perhaps 200,000 inhabitants.

Then the Spanish came. In 1519, twenty-seven years after Columbus arrived in the Americas, Hernán Cortés landed in Yucatán with just 600 soldiers plus a few cannons and horses. They marched inland, gaining allies as they went along among indigenous peoples who resented being ruled by the Aztecs. Within two years Cortés and the Spaniards ruled Mexico. They had conquered the Aztec Empire and devastated their great capital.

It was in that destruction that modern Mexico was born. The influence of the Aztecs and other indigenous people did not disappear even though untold numbers were killed. But neither can Mexico be recognized today without the Spanish influence.

Spain ruled for three centuries. Then in 1810 Mexicans began a struggle for independence from colonial Spain, much like the United States had fought for its own independence from Great Britain. In 1821 Mexico finally became an independent nation.

The newly born republic faced many difficulties. There was much poverty, especially among descendants of indigenous peoples; most of the wealth and political power was in the hands of a small elite of Spanish ancestry. To make things worse, Mexico lost almost half of its territory to the United States in a war that lasted from 1846 to 1848. Many still resent the loss of territory, which accounts for lingering anti-American sentiments among some Mexicans. The country was later occupied by France, but under national hero Benito Juárez Mexico regained its independence in 1867.

The next turning point in Mexican history came in 1911, when a revolution meant to help the millions of Mexicans stuck in poverty began against dictator Porfirio Díaz. There was violence and fighting until 1929, when Plutarco Elías Calles founded what was to become the *Partido Revolucionario Institucional*. It brought stability as well as economic progress. Yet millions of Mexicans remained in poverty, and as time went on PRI rulers became increasingly corrupt.

It was the desire of the people of Mexico to trust someone other than the candidate of PRI that resulted in the election of Fox. And so this nation of more than 100 million, with its ancient heritage, its diverse mestizo culture, its grinding poverty, and its glorious arts, stands on the brink of a new era. Modern Mexico is seeking a place as the leader of all Latin America, an ally of the United States, and an important voice in global politics. For that to happen, Mexico must narrow the gap between the rich and poor and bring more people in the middle class. It will be interesting to watch as Fox and the Mexican people work to bring their country into the first rank of nations.

The Olmecs, an early Mexican tribe, carved this giant head out of rock and placed it in their sacred city at La Venta, Mexico. Mexico has a rich cultural heritage, drawing on both native and Spanish traditions.

NATIVE AND SPANISH GOVERNMENT UNTIL 1810

The complex story of Mexico's governments began thousands of years ago, long before the political parties and the revolutions of the modern era. Starting around 1200 B.C., the native peoples of the area we now call Mexico ruled over great empires. These peoples included the Olmecs, the Zapotecs, the Maya, the Toltecs, and the Aztecs.

The Olmec civilization dominated the southern coast of the Gulf of Mexico from about 1200 to 400 B.C. Historians did not know about this culture until the 19th century, when a farmer in the state of Veracruz found the first of several huge stone heads, representing Olmec rulers. The Olmecs carried on trade with other parts of Mexico, and built important political centers at San Lorenzo and La Venta. From about 500 B.C. until A.D. 700, the Zapotecs ruled from Monte Albán in Oaxaca, a southern state on the Pacific coast. Then the empires of the Maya and Teotihuacán dominated Mexico from about A.D. 250 to 900. The Maya ruled over the Yucatán Peninsula in southeastern Mexico. They built great pyramids, temples, observatories, and other buildings at centers such as Chichén Itzá and Tikal. Their kings inherited the right to rule from their ancestors. A number of Mayan rulers were women.

At Teotihuacán, near Mexico City in north central Mexico, a great civilization existed from about 150 B.C. until A.D. 750. At its height, Teotihuacán's population may have been as high as 200,000. Its great structures, like the Temple of the Feathered Serpent and the Moon Pyramid, can still be seen today. The rulers of Teotihuacán did not record their names or accomplishments. Instead, they honored their gods in the city's many works of art.

The Toltec empire, which began around A.D. 900, ruled mainly from Tula, near Mexico City. However, the influence of the Toltecs can be found in many different areas of Mexico. They were the most warlike civilization that had yet appeared in *Mesoamerica*. Their empire declined around 1250.

The Aztec empire was the last great native empire in Mexico's history. The empire included a large part of south central Mexico. The Aztecs built a great city at Tenochtitlán, where Mexico City is today. By 1500, they controlled Mexico. Even in the areas of Mexico where they did not have direct influence, the other native cultures declined because the Aztec empire was so dominant. The Aztecs had a carefully structured class system. At the top was the king, whom the Aztecs believed was a god. The Aztec helped to keep their large empire together by marrying members of the royal family to women from far-off parts of the empire.

The name "Mexico" comes from the Mexica, the most powerful tribe included in the group of tribes known as the Aztecs.

The Toltec civilization predated the Aztecs and is believed to have been artistically and culturally sophisticated. These Toltec statues are located in what was once their capital, known as Tula (Place of the Reeds).

At the height of the empire, Tenochtitlán was one of the largest cities in the world.

In 1519, the course of Mexican history changed forever. Since the 1490s, the Spanish had been steadily expanding their influence in the Americas. Their settlements on the islands of the Caribbean made it easy for them to expand into Mexico. In February 1519, the *conquistador* Hernán Cortés set sail with a large army for the mainland of Mexico. He then marched to Tenochtitlán. The Spanish took the city quite easily, in part

When he sailed to Mexico in 1519, Hernán Cortés brought 16 horses with him, as well as his army. Before that, there were no horses in the Americas. The descendants of those horses, and others that the Spanish later brought to America, can be found in North and South America today.

These Mayan ruins loom over the coast of Quintana Roo. Unlike many other ancient Mexican societies, the Mayan culture has never completely died out. There are currently about 6 million Mayan Mexicans who speak the language and live according to some of the traditional customs.

because the Aztec emperor, Montezuma, thought that Cortés might be a god. The Aztec revolted in 1520, but the Spanish defeated them after getting more reinforcements. By August 1521, the Spanish had complete control of Tenochtitlán.

The Spanish built Mexico City on the site of Tenochtitlán. They called their new possession the **viceroyalty** of New Spain. The rulers of New Spain were officials appointed by the Spanish royal family. The viceroy controlled the central areas, while governors were appointed to look after outlying areas. New Spain society placed white people from Spain, or *peninsulares*, in the position of greatest power, while their descendants, called *criollos* (or creoles), were next in social standing. Below the criollos came African slaves and people of mixed race. These included the *mestizos*, who were of mixed Spanish and native race. The

Montezuma II, the last king of the Aztecs, reigned for less than 20 years before Spanish conquistadors led by Hernán Cortés conquered Mexico. Some aspects of the Aztec culture have been integrated into modern Mexican life, from food and religious beliefs to language.

MONTEZUMA.

Catholic Church, which was the official religion, influenced most aspects of society.

From the 1760s onward, King Charles III of Spain felt that the New Spain colony had become too self-reliant. He wanted to increase his own control over New Spain and collect more taxes from the colony. The king created more positions in the government, all of which were given to peninsulares. The changes in the organization of the government were called the Bourbon Reforms. In most cases, the criollos still supported rule by Spain. However, matters were complicated when Napoleon I of France invaded Spain in 1808 and ***deposed*** the royal family. Since the people of Spain were now acting for themselves against the French, many inhabitants of New Spain felt that they, too, should be able to govern themselves. The stage was set for a widespread movement toward independence.

THE ROAD TO INDEPENDENCE

By 1810, there was major unrest in Mexico. Many *criollos* called for increased independence from Spain. Others wanted to maintain the ***status quo***. The *peninsulares* were divided on what to do. When the *ayuntamiento*, or municipal council, of Mexico City called for self-government, the viceroy supported the council's demands. But some of the *peninsulares* overthrew the viceroy and stopped his movement toward change in the government.

By this time, many political societies existed in Mexico. Some were more active than others in demanding independence. One very active society existed in Querétaro, a small province in central Mexico. The people there planned to rise against the government in December 1910. However, the officials heard about the plan and started to arrest

The Monument to Independence stands in Mexico City. Although the War for Independence won Mexico freedom from Spanish rule, the aftermath left the country fragmented and chaotic.

18

members of the society in September. On September 16, the criollo priest Miguel Hidalgo y Costilla took control of the independence movement at a small town called Dolores. He delivered a speech known as the *"Grito de Dolores"* (Cry of Dolores) to the native and mestizo members of his church. In it, he called on the natives especially to rise up against the Spanish officials who took their land and ruled them in an unjust manner. He also gave them permission to use violence if necessary, though permission was probably not needed.

After a few weeks, Hidalgo, carrying a picture of the Virgin Mary for inspiration, commanded an army of 80,000. The church *excommunicated* him. In reply, Hidalgo announced that slavery was banned. However, the royalists (those who supported Spain's rule) soon started to win victories over the rebels. They captured Hidalgo in the spring of 1811, along with other leaders of the rebellion. At his trial, Hidalgo seemed to regret his rebellion. He called it "an inconceivable act of indiscretion and a frenzy." The royalists removed Hidalgo from the priesthood and executed him on July 30, 1811.

For the time being, the independence movement seemed all but gone. However, by 1813, another priest had taken the lead in the movement. His name was José María Morelos y Pavón, and he was a mestizo. Hidalgo had asked Morelos to organize the rebellion in southern

Even before his revolt began, the Mexican Inquisition followed Hidalgo's actions carefully. The Inquisition existed in both Spain and Mexico. It was meant to make people follow Roman Catholicism and to keep the church from becoming corrupt. The Inquisition became famous for its unjust trials. It also became very political, especially in Mexico.

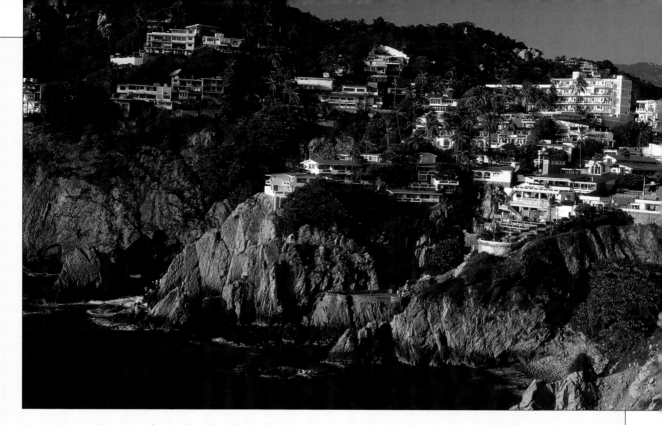

In 1810, when José María Morelos decided to join Hidalgo's revolt, his first assignment was to capture the port of Acapulco, Guerrero. Though he did not succeed in repeated campaigns on the city, he helped to advance the revolution over five years of fighting. His execution in 1815 was a serious blow to the revolution, however, and marked the end of the organized movement.

Mexico, and now Morelos operated from the southern state of Guerrero. He showed great skill in organizing rebels from all levels of society into a disciplined army. This army captured many key areas of Mexico.

In September 1813, Morelos asked ***delegates*** from the areas controlled by the rebels to meet for a conference where they would discuss a new constitution. At this conference, Morelos explained his

The attitude and determination of Miguel Hidalgo y Costilla inspired a fervor in the villagers of New Spain that led to the War for Independence. On Mexico's Independence Day each year, statues of Hidalgo across the country are decorated with red, white, and green flowers to honor his memory.

ideas for the new Mexico. It would be a *republic*. Everyone who lived in Mexico would have the same rights, regardless of their race. Also, Morelos wanted the large properties belonging to the church and to rich landowners to be broken up. On November 6, the conference went so far as to declare Mexico's independence.

The royalists fought back, though. They executed Morelos in 1815. By 1816, royalist forces controlled most parts of Mexico again. In Spain, the king was back in power. He declared that the constitution was not valid. But in 1820, the Spanish monarchy was once again shaken by revolt. The king had to put a liberal constitution into effect. Among other points, the constitution allowed for freedom of speech and gave less power to the church than it previously had. Seeing the changes taking place in Spain, the Mexican criollos decided that they wanted independence. However, they did not want a complete change. They wanted an independent nation ruled over by a monarch.

Things did not work out as planned by the conservative criollos. They asked Agustín de Iturbide, an officer who had fought against the rebels in the past, to help bring in this new government. They wanted this done by military force. Instead, Iturbide met with Vicente Guerrero, the rebel leader. The two leaders then joined forces. On February 24, 1821, they signed the Plan of Iguala.

The Plan included three main points. First, Mexico would become an independent nation under the rule of a monarch from a European royal family. A junta, or government council, would rule until they had a monarch. The **congress** would draw up a constitution. Second, Roman Catholicism would be the official religion. Third, all Mexican citizens were to be free and equal. Because of the three major guarantees in the Plan, the united forces were called the *Trigarante*.

The Mexican viceroy resigned, but Spain sent another viceroy, who chose to work with the new government. On September 28, 1821, Mexico declared its independence.

WARS AND REFORMS

To begin with, a junta dominated by conservative criollos ruled over Mexico. Iturbide was elected one of the leaders of the junta. However, no one from the European royalty wanted to become the ruler of Mexico. Iturbide, a vain and ambitious man, decided that he was the best ruler available. In May of 1822, he staged a *coup* and became the first emperor of Mexico.

While in power, Iturbide ruled over a huge territory. It included parts of the modern-day United States in the north, to Panama in the south. But many people were unhappy with Iturbide's rule. He wanted to be an emperor like Napoléon of France, and he wasted a lot of money to that end. Members of his court had to observe a certain code of conduct, which included kissing Iturbide's hand to show respect. Mexico suffered an economic decline under his leadership. In 1823, he resigned after a military revolt.

In this colored Mexican illustration, Agustin de Iturbide rides triumphantly into Mexico City in 1821. Iturbide, a Mexican military leader, became emperor of Mexico but his government soon fell during a revolt. He was exiled in 1823; when he returned a year later, Iturbude was captured and executed.

Mexico's first president was Guadalupe Victoria. In 1824, the constitution officially made Mexico a republic. The republic was divided into 19 states and four territories. The constitution also guaranteed freedom of speech and officially ended slavery. Each state had its own governor and *legislature*. The legislatures of each state elected the president and vice-president of Mexico.

Because of the ongoing struggle between liberals and conservatives, Mexico's government was unstable. In 1828, a conservative candidate won the presidential election. However, the liberals deposed the new president and put Vicente Guerrero in his place. Guerrero had been the rebel leader when Mexico became independent. He became president mainly because of Antonio López de Santa Anna, a general who had helped overthrow Iturbide.

Santa Anna himself became the president in 1833. He was to be the president 11 times between 1833 and 1855. During that time, he changed his political leanings more than once. In 1834, he made himself a *dictator*. The Mexican states became military departments. They were completely under the control of Santa Anna.

At this point in time, Texas was part of Mexico. Texas also included modern-day states such as California and New Mexico. Although it was part of Mexico, Texas was home to many Americans. The Texans were unhappy with many of Mexico's policies. They became even more dissatisfied in 1836, when the constitution took away the *autonomy* of the states, including Texas. As a result, war broke out.

Mexico defeated the Texan forces at the battle of the Alamo just days after Texas's declaration of independence. However, Santa Anna

Agustin de Iturbide (left) tried to model his government after that of Napoleon Bonaparte, the former emperor of France. However, this did not sit well with the people, and Iturbide's government fell within a few years.

suffered a defeat at San Jacinto soon after. The Texan army captured Santa Anna and held him prisoner. So that the Texans would let him go, Santa Anna signed an agreement to let Texas become independent. The government and people of Mexico were angry at Santa Anna's action. They did not recognize the independence of Texas, though other countries did.

Between 1836 and 1845, Mexico was busy with difficulties within its

In Texas, Antonio López de Santa Anna is best known for leading his troops to victory against the Alamo defenders. Santa Anna was known throughout Mexico at different times as a military leader, president, and emperor.

own borders. Then, early in 1845, the United States decided to *annex* Texas. Mexico was determined to protect its border. In 1846, the U.S. Army advanced south into territory claimed both by the United States and Mexico. When Mexican soldiers fought back, America declared war. Meanwhile, different Mexican politicians struggled for power, weakening the country.

The United States won the battle for Chihuahua, in northern Mexico, in early 1847. Later that year, the battle of Buena Vista ended without a victory for either side. However, both sides announced to their nations that they had won. Santa Anna withdrew his army to Mexico City. U.S. forces then landed at Veracruz, on the south coast of the Gulf of Mexico. They captured the city and marched to Mexico City. The last desperate battles of the war took place around the capital city in August and September of 1847. Far more Mexicans than Americans lost their lives. On February 2, 1848, Mexico signed a treaty giving the territory that included Arizona, California, and New Mexico to the United States. The signing of this treaty ended the war.

As a result of the war with the United States, Mexico lost half of its territory. The costs of warfare also left the government with great financial difficulties. Despite this, for the next five years, Mexico enjoyed a fairly peaceful time. However, the struggle for political power within Mexico continued between the liberals and the conservatives. The liberals, including many politically active *mestizos*, wanted a more American-style government. They wanted equal rights for all and new business ventures that would help the growth of the economy. The conservatives wanted to keep the church and the military in their positions of power. They did not want to allow too much power to the "lower classes," which mainly included native people and people of mixed race.

During the war and until 1853, Mexico was once again under a *federal* government. But in 1853, Santa Anna took power for the last time as a dictator. He gave himself the title of Most Serene Highness, and led a wasteful lifestyle. He also taxed the people of Mexico heavily. His *cabinet* was made up of men who insisted on total government control of almost all aspects of life. There was no

The battle of the Alamo is one of the most famous battles in U.S. history. When Mexican forces attacked the fort at the Alamo, they greatly outnumbered the small American force. There were 187 American soldiers and about 15 civilians at the fort. The soldiers included the famous frontiersmen Davy Crockett and James Bowie. After holding off the Mexicans for several days, all the Texan soldiers were killed. However, 600 Mexicans also died. At the battle of San Jacinto soon after, the rallying cry throughout Texas was "Remember the Alamo!"

28

congress, and the ordinary people had no right to political involvement.

Revolts started to break out, especially in the state of Guerrero. The rebel leader there was Juan Alvarez, a liberal criollo. Elsewhere, a group of liberals worked to organize the overthrow of Santa Anna's dictatorship. Among others, their leaders were Melchor Ocampo, a mestizo, and Benito Juárez, a native of the Zapotec tribe. Both had been exiled to Louisiana by Santa Anna, along with other liberals who were considered dangerous. After a year and a half of civil war, the liberals took control in 1855.

Alvarez temporarily became the president of Mexico. Juárez, Ocampo, and others took important positions in the government. In 1857, the new government introduced a new constitution. It was completely liberal, for the first time in the history of Mexico. The constitution upheld equality and free speech. Also, it put an end to special treatment in court for members of the clergy and the military.

The liberal government also introduced many controversial reforms. One of the most important reforms involved breaking up and selling the huge areas of land owned by the church. Unfortunately for the native peoples, the new laws also broke up their *communal* lands.

The reforms resulted in a conservative revolt in 1858. Juárez left Mexico City, but the liberals declared him their new president

The final battle of the Mexican-American war was at Mexico City's Chapultepec Castle, on September 13, 1847. The last Mexican soldiers to stand against the Americans were a group of young men now known as the "Niños Héroes," or Heroic Children. There is a monument to them at the site of the battle.

After Santa Anna was removed from power in 1854, Benito Juárez had the task of reforming Mexico's government. When Juarez became president, he tried to stabilize Mexico's economy by creating infrastructure, such as railroads and schools.

and set up a government in Veracruz. Meanwhile, the conservatives named their own president in Mexico City. The revolt led into the War of the Reform, which lasted from 1858 to 1861. It was a very bitter war, with many deaths and atrocities on both sides. In 1859, Juárez confiscated a huge amount of church property. He did this to stop the church from giving financial support to the conservatives. On January 1, 1861, the liberals captured Mexico City. In June, Juárez became the president of all Mexico.

A group of girls marches in a Cinco de Mayo parade in Puebla, Mexico. Cinco de Mayo (the Fifth of May) is one of Mexico's most famous holidays. On this day, Mexicans celebrate the Mexican army's victory over the French at the battle of Puebla in 1862.

EUROPEAN INTERVENTION AND ITS AFTERMATH

In 1861, Mexico's economy was in a terrible state. The government was heavily in debt to Britain, France, and Spain. Some of these debts went back almost 50 years. The largest debt by far was owed to Britain. In July 1861, Juárez declared that Mexico would stop payment of its debts for two years. During that time, the government would try to rebuild the economy. In October, Britain, France, and Spain signed an agreement, the Convention of London. In the Convention, they agreed to occupy Mexico and to make sure that their debts were paid off. The Spanish were the first to arrive, in December. British and French troops followed soon after.

Napoléon III was the French emperor at this time. A nephew of the famous Napoléon I, he was an extremely ambitious man. He wanted to establish a French empire even greater than his uncle's, one that would stretch around the world. It soon became obvious to the British and the Spanish that the French wanted to make Mexico part of their empire. In protest, Britain and Spain ordered their troops home in 1862. Meanwhile, the French troops advanced toward Mexico City. In May, they attacked Mexican forces at the city of Puebla. On May 5, the Mexicans won a major victory against the shocked French. This day, the "Cinco de Mayo" is still celebrated throughout Mexico.

However, many conservative Mexicans joined forces with the French. In 1863, the French rallied and took Mexico City. Juárez and his government decided to withdraw. The French asked the Austrian archduke Ferdinand Maximilian of Hapsburg to take the Mexican throne. In 1864, Maximilian arrived in Mexico.

Maximilian was still a young man when he came to the throne. He was also a very idealistic person. He wanted to help Mexico's cultural life, and also to assist the underprivileged members of society. For instance, he established laws about child labor. He also tried to guarantee equal rights for all. At least to begin with, many Mexicans seemed to support the new emperor. However, this apparent support was mainly a ploy by the French to make Maximilian happy about ruling over the Mexicans. Conflicts continued under the new leadership. Many liberals abandoned Juárez and went over to the French

"Life in Mexico is worth fighting for...the country and its people are much better than they are reputed to be, and you would be astonished at how well the Empress and I, completely Mexicanized by now, live among these people."
—Emperor Maximilian writing to a friend in 1866

Napoleon III, the nephew of Napoleon Bonaparte, capitalized on his respected name and became emperor of France for two decades. However, his rule ended similarly to Bonaparte's; he died in exile after being defeated in war.

side. Other liberals continued to wage guerilla warfare against the invaders and their supporters.

Maximilian's government was not a success, even though many ordinary Mexicans came to like him. The liberals were against him because the conservatives and French had put him in power and driven out the liberal government. At the same time, many conservatives did not like his leanings. They felt that his new constitution was much too liberal. Also, Maximilian would not return the church's property. Because of this, the church refused to cooperate with him.

Back in France, Napoléon was getting more and more concerned about the possibility of war in Europe. The United States, whose Civil War had just ended and which was no longer quite so distracted, also wanted the withdrawal of French troops from Mexico. The withdrawal took place in 1867, while the Juaristas (supporters of Juárez) took back huge areas of Mexico. Maximilian still wanted to support France, which had given him his position of power. He left Mexico City and went to Querétaro, where the last French troops on Mexican soil were located. There, the Juaristas captured him. Juárez had the unfortunate emperor tried and sentenced to death. A firing squad executed him on June 19, 1867.

Juárez won the presidential elections of 1867. The years from 1867 to 1871 were his third term as president, and many people felt that it was his most successful. During this time, Mexico was reasonably peaceful. Juárez wanted to introduce reforms that would make the presidency stronger. He felt that the congress had too much power, and that the government should be more centralized. Some people felt that Juárez was actually trying to make himself a dictator. He wanted to make changes to the old liberal constitution of 1857. The proposed changes included increased powers of **veto** for the president, and less power for regional governments. Juárez tried to have the people vote on these issues, but without success. However, he was able to work around what he saw as the constitution's limitations, so as to make some of the changes that he wanted.

Because there were many bandits in Mexico, and travel could be very dangerous, he strengthed the police forces in rural areas. The Juárez government also worked to improve the roads. They completed the railroad between Mexico City and Veracruz, which had been started in the 1830s.

In 1871, Juárez decided to run for president once again. Since he had already governed for three terms, he was really not supposed to run for office another time. Many liberals were not happy. It seemed that Juárez wanted to keep his position of power at all costs. One liberal said: "Today it is not the Constitution that the government defends, but the Presidential Chair."

Three candidates ran for the presidential office. Porfirio Díaz, a mestizo general who had distinguished himself in the Cinco de Mayo battle, was one of the other candidates. There was no clear majority, and the congress declared Juárez president. Díaz organized a revolt, which failed. In 1872, Juárez died suddenly of a heart attack.

In place of Juárez, Sebastián Lerdo became acting president. He won the election by a large majority. Lerdo had been the head of the Supreme Court under Juárez. Like Juárez, he worked to expand the country's railroads and to increase funding for schools.

When Benito Juárez decided to have Maximilian executed, the European nations were upset and outraged. Many prominent people, from the French author Victor Hugo to Queen Victoria, asked Juárez to change his mind. Juárez responded that if he did not have Maximilian executed, the people of Mexico would do so themselves.

Porfirio Díaz helped to overthrow Antonio López de Santa Anna's dictatorship and fought alongside Benito Juárez in the famous attack on May 5, 1862. He was president of Mexico for a total of 31 years, and his period of influence is generally referred to as the Porfiriato.

However, many liberals believed that he suffered from a haughty and superior attitude.

In 1876, Lerdo had himself reelected. In response, Porfirio Díaz issued the Plan of Tuxtepec. He argued in the Plan that Lerdo's reelection was unconstitutional. He also accused Lerdo of wasting Mexico's finances on railroad enterprises and denying the people the right to a fair vote. Díaz used these accusations as an excuse for an armed revolt. After defeating Lerdo's forces on November 16 at Tecoac, in the state of Tlaxcala, Díaz took Mexico a few days later. He was duly elected as president soon after.

A group of steel mill workers on the job in Michoacan, Mexico. Building steel mills was part of Porfirio Díaz's plan to improve Mexico's economy by creating more industrial jobs.

THE PORFIRIATO AND THE REVOLUTION

Despite his claims that he was against reelection, Porfirio Díaz remained in power until 1911. In 1880, he helped one of his generals, Manuel Gonzalez, to become president. This move was a ploy to make it look as though he were obeying the law against reelection. Díaz acted through Gonzalez as ruler, though he also allowed the new president to do things on his own initiative. However, this presidential term was marked by corruption. After 1884, when Díaz was once again openly the president, he had the laws about reelection changed. Now, all government officials were allowed to stay in their positions of power for unlimited periods of time. During Díaz's time in power, real elections more or less ceased to exist. Since it was decided in advance that Díaz would win, the elections were prearranged for show.

Díaz's rule is known as the *Porfiriato*. Many Mexicans view his time in office as a dictatorship. He did not abolish the rights laid down in the constitution or take away the right to vote, but he did reserve complete political power to himself. He was, however, a deeply patriotic man who wanted to bring peace and order to his country, which had been torn apart by conflicts for so long. The slogans of his *regime* were "Ordered Progress" and "Less Politics, More Administration." Díaz believed that he could use any means necessary to achieve peace. He never hesitated to execute those that he saw as enemies. To help control Mexico's bandit problem, he made some of the country's worst bandits into members of the rural police. These men were prepared to kill anyone who was causing a problem. Many foreign visitors to the country were impressed by the apparent peace that the country was experiencing under Díaz. A U.S. travel writer of the time called the rural police "picturesque," which was not very accurate.

Díaz encouraged foreign investment, which stimulated the economy. Many people were unhappy, however, because so much of Mexico's resources were controlled by foreigners, especially Americans. Díaz himself recognized some of the problems with this policy. He reportedly said: "Poor Mexico, so far from God and so near to the United States."

Mexico became a much more industrialized country. More railroads were built, as well as silver, gold, and copper mines and the first steel mill in Latin America. Díaz also encouraged foreigners to

Before becoming a politician, Porfirio Díaz studied to be a priest, as well as studying law. However, he dropped out before finishing the courses for either profession. He was a poor writer, and he never read books.

The tumultuous political climate of Mexico in the early 20th century meant that no ruler stayed in power for very long. Francisco Indalecio Madero managed to wrest the presidency away from Porfirio Diaz, but was overthrown himself after only two years.

move to Mexico and work there. This policy was in line with the view of many in Díaz's government, that the natives of Mexico were lazy and incompetent. Díaz surrounded himself with a group called the *"cientificos,"* or scientific thinkers. They believed that social and economic advancement could be achieved through logic and the study of statistics and the trends that they revealed. They also thought that those who were white or part white were superior to the native peoples.

During Díaz's regime, most of the native peoples' communal land was taken away from them. The natives had to work on large ranches called *haciendas*. They received low wages, inadequate food, and poor treatment. There were many peasant uprisings, which were quickly crushed.

Emiliano Zapata led a large-scale peasant revolt in South Mexico in the early part of the 20th century. Still one of Mexico's most important historical figures, his principles live on through the Zapatista Army of National Liberation (EZLN).

There were also good things about the Díaz government. A lot of money was spent on education—although school was still not available to nearly enough people. The country was also relatively peaceful.

However, the Porfiriato had many problems. Despite the apparent peace and order, crime increased. Life expectancy was low and infant mortality was high. The gap between the rich and the poor increased, because the new wealth and material advantages only reached the rich. Díaz's policies contradicted each other in many ways. His government was supposed to be a democracy, but it actually functioned as a dictatorship. Díaz had control over most aspects of life in Mexico, for what he felt was the good of the country.

During the 1900s, Mexico suffered economically, and there was a serious economic depression in 1907. Díaz came under increasing criticism, even from his friends and allies. In the same year, Díaz gave an interview for a popular American magazine. In this interview, he stated that he would retire at the end of his current term. He also claimed that he would welcome an opposition party. When the interview became public, some politicians took Díaz at his word.

One of them was Francisco Madero. He was a politician from one of Mexico's richest families. Madero was an eccentric, who often tried to communicate with the dead. During one of these attempts, he claimed to have received a message from Benito Juárez. The spirit of Juárez apparently said that he had chosen Madero to be the next leader of Mexico.

Madero asked for Díaz's permission to stand for election. He wanted a return to a real democracy, including open elections. Díaz actually had no intention of stepping down or of allowing an opposition party to take over. He refused to let Madero run for president. However, in 1909, Madero formed a political party called the Anti-Reelectionist Party. He traveled around the country to raise support, and was very successful. Alarmed by this threat, Díaz made up an excuse in 1910 to put Madero into jail. In the same year, he had himself reelected as usual.

Madero was in jail in San Luis Potosí. He

> Emiliano Zapata's rallying cry was *"Tierra y Libertad,"* which means "Land and Freedom."

was allowed to move around the town with a bodyguard. In October 1910, he broke away from his guards on horseback and fled to Texas. There, he made his Plan of San Luis public. The Plan declared that Díaz's reelection was not valid, and that the time had come for a revolution.

The Revolution officially began on November 20, 1910, with guerilla fighting in scattered areas. During the next weeks, increasing resistance sprang up throughout Mexico. People from all walks of life joined the Revolution. Besides Madero, two of the most important rebel leaders were Emiliano Zapata and Francisco "Pancho" Villa. Villa had previously lived as a bandit, while Zapata, who was a farmer and horse trainer, took up the cause of peasants and natives. He helped to take back portions of land that had been seized from the peasants.

Meanwhile, support for Díaz was diminishing. After months of fighting, he allowed his representatives to sign a treaty with his enemies in May 1911. Part of the agreement was that Díaz would resign. However, the old dictator continued to resist. When it became public knowledge that Díaz had agreed to resign, crowds gathered in Mexico City to demand that he step down immediately. Díaz ordered his troops to fire on the crowds, and 200 people died. On May 25, however, Díaz gave in. He announced his resignation and left the country.

In November, Madero became the officially elected president. He would hold the position until early 1913, but Madero was not able to create a strong government. He found himself at the head of a completely disunited Mexico. Madero made several mistakes. He appointed family members to high positions in the government that they were not qualified for. He also paid little attention to the revolutionary

One of the most influential revolutionaries of his time, Francisco "Pancho" Villa was considered a champion of the Mexican Revolution. In 1966 he was declared a national hero for his efforts to improve the government and society of Mexico.

leaders, such as Zapata and Villa, who had helped him to power. Madero even allowed important members of the Porfiriato government to keep high political positions. Zapata and his followers, the Zapatistas, turned against Madero. They accused him of making promises about land reform and not following through on them. Workers went on strike when they did not get better working conditions.

Madero did work to improve voting procedures. He also directed money toward better methods of agriculture, education, railroads, and highways. However, there were several major revolts by conservatives and former allies during his time in office. In 1913, these revolts culminated in the *"Decena Trágica"*—the Ten Tragic Days.

On February 9, 1913, two of the leaders of revolts against Madero were freed from jail in Mexico City by supporters from the army. One of them was Félix Díaz, a nephew of Porfirio Díaz. They had been plotting this latest revolt while in jail. Madero appointed one of his generals, Victoriano Huerta, to lead his troops in fighting back the rebels. Civil war raged in the streets for days, killing and wounding thousands. Huerta then joined forces with Félix Díaz. He did so at the prompting of the American ambassador to Mexico, who wanted to protect American foreign interests in Mexico. He took Madero prisoner and had himself declared

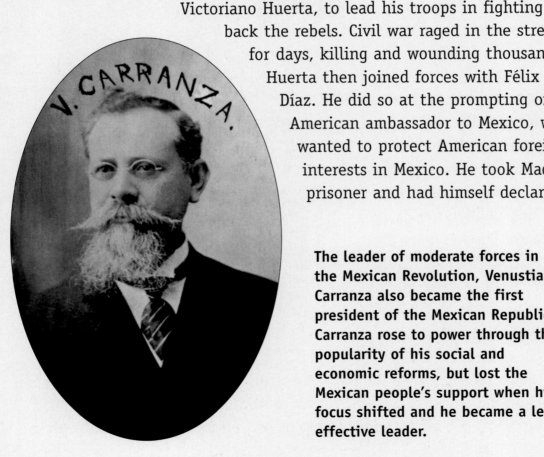

The leader of moderate forces in the Mexican Revolution, Venustiano Carranza also became the first president of the Mexican Republic. Carranza rose to power through the popularity of his social and economic reforms, but lost the Mexican people's support when his focus shifted and he became a less effective leader.

president. On February 21, Madero and his vice-president reportedly died when some of their supporters tried to free them. They were actually executed.

Huerta did not claim to have taken power for the good of Mexico. In fact, he established a dictatorship. In the south, the Zapatistas fought back against the new government. In the north, a state governor named Venustiano Carranza formed the Constitutional Army of the North, to fight against Huerta's denial of the constitution. The United States sided against Huerta. In April 1914, U.S. forces prevented an arms shipment for Huerta from landing at Veracruz, and occupied the city. Most Mexicans, not just supporters of Huerta, were angry at this intervention. However, the United States did not take their intervention any further. Still, with too many military fronts to deal with, Huerta resigned in July. Carranza occupied Mexico City.

The various rebel forces simply could not put their differences aside. Threatened by Villa and Zapata, Carranza withdrew his government from Mexico City to Veracruz. Zapata's army, dressed in their distinctive **sombreros**, occupied Mexico City in December 1914. Villa's army followed them. However, the rebel leaders soon moved out of the capital again. During 1915, vicious fighting continued between Carranza's forces and those of Villa and Zapata. By 1916, though, Carranza seemed to be in a definitive position of power.

Like many Mexicans, Plutarco Elías Calles entered politics only after Porfirio Diaz's 31-year rule ended. Calles was elected president of Mexico in 1924, and set about working to help small farmers and workers prosper, as well as organizing a modern banking system for the country.

FROM THE CONSTITUTION OF 1917 TO THE 21ST CENTURY

I n February 1917, the Carranza government adopted a new constitution. The Constitution of 1917 focused on the concerns of the middle classes. One of the articles stated that all of Mexico's natural resources belonged to the people of Mexico. This was a way of minimizing foreign involvement in Mexico. The constitution also made provisions to return communal lands to the native peoples. It included basic rights such as education and good working conditions for all. The constitution limited the power of the Catholic Church and allowed for freedom of religion.

Carranza himself would have preferred a more conservative constitution, but he accepted the Constitution of 1917. After officially becoming the president in March, he failed to enforce many of the ideals outlined in the constitution. He kept his presidency until 1920.

During that time, he resisted the efforts of trade unions to improve the lives of workers, and he did little to put the new land reforms into practice. He once said: "In order to be free, it is not enough to want it but one also has to know how to be free." His idea of "freedom" was still too close to a dictatorship for many Mexicans.

Zapata continued fighting for his peasants during the Carranza years. Thousands of innocent people died because the government suspected them of aiding Zapata. Finally, Zapata was shot and killed on April 10, 1919. However, Carranza himself died during a revolt in 1920, at the end of his time in office. Alvaro Obregón, who led the revolt, became the next president.

Obregón did far more to put the constitution into practice than Carranza had. His government was quite moderate. Although he furthered the land reforms, giving back land to the native peoples, he also encouraged foreign investment. One of his main concerns was that Mexico stay relatively peaceful during his time in office. He encouraged cooperation between the different levels of society, but he also made sure that the lower classes did not have a chance to become too independent or to see too many of their revolutionary ideals realized. The official in charge of education under Obregón, José Vasconcelos, greatly increased spending on education. He also worked to stimulate culture and to improve Mexico's sense of its own identity.

In 1924, Plutarco Elías Calles became the new president in a peaceful

> **"I was responsible for the helm but not the storm."**
> **—President López Portillo on September 1, 1982, refusing to take responsibility for the economic problems caused by the failure of the oil industry**

Alvaro Obregon was elected twice to the Mexican presidency. His most notable accomplishment was helping to restore order to the country after its destructive civil war.

transition of power. Calles had been the governor of the state of Sonora, where he had introduced many educational reforms. As president of Mexico, he worked on improving the economy. He founded the Bank of Mexico and the National Bank of Agricultural Credit. The National Bank of Agricultural Credit helped farming societies on the local and state level. However, some of Calles's policies were very controversial. He made primary education **secular** rather than religious. He also expelled foreign-born priests and limited the activities of the Catholic Church in other ways. In 1926, these policies provoked the Cristero Rebellion. Priests refused to perform baptisms, marriages, and funerals. Some peasants rose up in rebellion. They became known as Cristeros because of their rallying cry, *"Viva Cristo Rey"* (Long Live Christ the King). The rebellion lasted for years, and many died.

When Obregón was reelected in 1928, a religious fanatic assassinated him soon afterward. Because of the uncertainty about who would be the next president, Mexico seemed to be on the verge of another crisis. Calles announced that he would retire from politics. But he really intended to rule behind the scenes. He called himself the Supreme Chief. He also

The Zapatista National Liberation Army (EZLN) is a guerilla group that has organized armed resistance against the Mexican government. This photo of a Zapatista was taken in 1995 in the Chiapas province of Mexico.

announced the founding of the Partido Nacional Revolucionario (PNR), or National Revolutionary Party. The PNR was a way of bringing together all the major political parties in Mexico. The idea was that under the PNR, the parties would be united for the common good of Mexico. Because of its wide-ranging control over political affairs, the PNR would determine the presidency. The irony of the PNR was that, despite its name, it was not very revolutionary. It encouraged a more conservative outlook.

The next president, Lázaro Cárdenas, soon escaped the control of Calles and sent him into exile. Cárdenas became popular because he handed over a lot of land to natives and peasants. He also allowed the formation of a large workers' union, the Confederation of Mexican Workers. This union allowed workers to defend their rights and fight for higher wages. The workers' situation improved even more in 1938, when Cárdenas took away the property of the foreign oil companies and gave them back to Mexico. In the same year, conservatives and Catholics founded the Partido de Acción Nacional (PAN), or National Action Party. This party would eventually play an important role in Mexican politics.

Mexican government became increasingly conservative in the 1940s. The country was more peaceful than it had ever been since the beginning of independence. Education became much more widely available than it had been before, as well as health care. The government lowered its military spending. However, through the 1940s and '50s, the country's resources also came to be under the control of a smaller number of powerful people. Thus, the difference between the rich and the poor became even greater. Foreign investment increased, creating new jobs for some but putting others out of business. Mexico also had an extremely high birth rate at this time, which created employment and housing problems.

In the 1960s, dissatisfaction grew with the ruling party, now called the Partido Revolucionario Institucional (PRI), or Institutional Revolutionary Party. Many students and activists felt that the government was too repressive. It seemed as though the PRI wanted to keep its *monopoly* over the country at all costs. An example of this was in 1965, when PAN won local elections in certain areas. The PRI government, under the president Díaz Ordaz, declared that the elections were not valid. In 1968, students rioted around the time of the Olympic Games in Mexico City. During one very large riot, soldiers fired on the students and killed over 300.

Mexico, along with other parts of the world, suffered a *recession* in the 1970s. The country also continued to experience high birth rates, as well as a shortage of *maize*, a very important Mexican food. The population of Mexico City exploded. Extreme poverty became common. Problems continued in the early 1980s, when the government invested huge sums of money in the production and selling of oil to other countries. When other foreign sellers offered the buyers a better deal, the value of the *peso* dropped enormously. The crisis also put Mexico deep in debt. The government worked hard to improve the economy during the 1980s, but the government's efforts were weakened by its own corruption.

In the late '80s, the PRI was more and more divided. In 1988, the ruling party gained only a tiny majority in the election. PAN became an increasingly important and popular party.

The early years of the 1990s were fairly uneventful in Mexican politics. The president, Carlos Salinas de Gortari, managed to have debt payments to other countries reduced. The economy improved a great deal during these years. However, the political events of 1994 shook all Mexico. In January, Zapatista rebels captured several towns in the state of Chiapas. They were protesting the start of the North American Free Trade Agreement (NAFTA), which they felt would make exploitation of Mexican workers and peasants by the United States much easier. The standoff ended quite soon, and troops took back the captured towns. But in March, the PRI's candidate for the presidency was assassinated. It was the first assassination in Mexican politics in over 50 years. Later that year, another important PRI official was shot and killed. Ernesto Zedillo became the new president. Through the final years of the 1990s, PAN continued to gain popularity.

July 2000 marked one of the biggest political upsets in Mexico's history. In the elections, Vicente Fox of PAN defeated the PRI candidate and became the president of Mexico. Since the founding in 1929 of the party that became the PRI, all of Mexico's presidents had been PRI candidates. Fox, who had been a state governor before becoming the president, won 43 percent of the vote. Thus, PAN does not have a majority in the government, since several other political parties won the other 57 percent of the vote. However, many Mexicans feel that Fox's election is a positive sign in Mexico's recent history. Before being elected, Fox promised to fight corruption in the government and to work at improving Mexico's economy. Under his government, many people think that Mexico enters the 21st century with a renewed sense of hope.

Vicente Fox was elected president of Mexico in 2000. Fox was the first president in seven decades who was not a member of the Party of the Institutionalized Revolution (PRI).

CHRONOLOGY

1200–400 B.C.	Olmecs rule the southern coast of the Gulf of Mexico.
500 B.C.–A.D. 700	The Zapotecs rule part of Mexico.
150 B.C.–A.D. 750	The Teotihuacán civilization exists in Mexico.
250–900	Mayans rule in Mexico.
900–1250	Toltecs rule in Mexico.
1325–1519	Aztec dominance in Mexico.
1519	Hernán Cortés arrives in Mexico with a large army.
1521	Cortés takes the Aztec capital of Tenochtitlán.
1807	The French occupy Spain and take the king of Spain prisoner.
1810	Miguel Hidalgo y Costilla rallies natives and mestizos to rebellion with his "Grito de Dolores."
1813	José María Morelos y Pavón organizes a rebellion.
1821	Agustín de Iturbide and Vicente Guerrero join forces to make Mexico independent.
1833	Antonio López de Santa Anna becomes president.
1836	The United States and Mexico fight important battles at the Alamo and San Jacinto.
1846	The United States declares war on Mexico.
1848	Mexico hands over Texas and other modern-day states to the United States.
1854	A liberal revolt drives Santa Anna out of power. Benito Juárez and others lead the new government.
1858	Juárez flees Mexico City after a conservative revolt. The War of the Reform begins.
1861	Juárez becomes president once again.
1862	The French, British and Spanish occupy Veracruz.

56

1864 The French, along with Mexican conservatives, make Maximilian of Austria emperor of Mexico.

1867 The French withdraw from Mexico, and Maximilian is executed by Juárez's forces.

1876 Porfirio Díaz becomes president and dictator of Mexico.

1910 The Mexican Revolution begins under Francisco Madero, Emiliano Zapata, and Francisco "Pancho" Villa.

1911 Díaz resigns and leaves Mexico. Madero becomes president

1913 Victoriano Huerta deposes Madero and becomes president.

1914 Venustiano Carranza occupies Mexico City. The revolutionary forces struggle among themselves.

1917 The Carranza government adopts a new constitution.

1929 Plutarco Elías Calles forms the National Revolutionary Part (PNR), which eventually becomes the Institutional Revolutionary Party (PRI).

1938 Lázaro Cárdenas returns the property of foreign oil companies to the people of Mexico.

1968 Over 300 students die in a riot protesting the policies of the PRI government.

1988 The PRI wins its smallest majority yet in the elections.

1994 Zapatista rebels capture several towns in Chiapas.

2000 Vicente Fox of the National Action Party (PAN) becomes the president of Mexico.

2001 President Fox meets with U.S. President George W. Bush to discuss a cooperative relationship between the neighboring countries.

2002 Latin American leaders, including Mexico's Vicente Fox, meet in Argentina for the Global Alumni Conference.

GLOSSARY

Annex	To take over a territory and add it to one's own territory.
Autonomy	Self-government.
Cabinet	A committee of senior officials in a government.
Communal	Shared between members of a community.
Conquistador	Any one of the Spanish leaders of the conquest of the Americas in the 1500s.
Congress	A group, forming part of a government, that makes up laws and meets to make important decisions.
Coup	Violent overthrow of a government.
Delegate	Person sent as a representative.
Deposed	Overthrew a ruler.
Dictator	A ruler with absolute authority in any area.
Excommunicate	To cut off a person from the Church, not allowing them to participate in any of its activities.
Federal	Describing a government made up of states that mostly govern themselves but unite for certain purposes.
Legislature	Law-making body of a government.
Maize	The corn plant grown in North America, including Mexico.
Mesoamerica	Area including Mexico and most of Central America.
Monopoly	Complete control.
Peso	Money of Mexico and several countries in Central and South America.
Recession	Decline in economic activity.

58

Regime   Rule or government.

Republic   A state where the people participate in the government as well as the official rulers.

Secular   Not religious.

Sombreros   Broad-brimmed Mexican hats.

Status quo   Unchanging state of affairs.

Veto   When a ruler or a group in government reserves the right to reject a decision.

Viceroyalty   A colony or province of a country ruled over by a monarch. The viceroyalty itself is governed by an official appointed by the monarch.

FURTHER READING

Carew-Miller, Anna. *Famous People of Mexico*. Philadelphia: Mason Crest Publishers, 2003.

Fehrenbach, T. R. *Fire and Blood, a History of Mexico*. New York: Da Capo Press, 1995.

Foster, Lynn V. *A Brief History of Mexico*. New York: Facts On File, 1997.

Franz, Carl. *The People's Guide to Mexico*. Emeryville, Calif.: Publishers Group West, 1995.

Goodwin, William. *Mexico: Modern Nations of the World*. San Diego: Lucent Press, 1999.

Hunter, Amy N. *The History of Mexico*. Philadelphia: Mason Crest Publishers, 2003.

Kimmel, Eric A. *Montezuma and the Fall of the Aztecs*. New York: Holiday House, 2000.

Krauze, Enrique. *Mexico: Biography of Power*. New York: HarperCollins Publishers, 1997.

O'Reilly, James and Larry Habegger. *Travelers' Tales: Mexico*. Sebastopol, Calif.: Travelers' Tales, 1994.

Meyer, Michael C. and William H. Beezley, eds. *The Oxford History of Mexico*. New York: Oxford University Press, 2000.

Ruiz, Ramón Eduardo. *Triumphs and Tragedy: A History of the Mexican People*. New York: W. W. Norton & Company, 1992.

Rummel, Jack. *Mexico*. Philadelphia: Chelsea House Publishers, 1999.

Warburton, Lois. *World History Series—Aztec Civilization*. San Diego: Lucent Press, 1995.

Werner, Michael. *The History of Mexico: History, Culture, and Society*. Chicago: Fitzroy Dearborn Publishers, 1997.

Williams, Colleen Madonna Flood. *The Geography of Mexico*. Philadelphia: Mason Crest Publishers, 2003.

INTERNET RESOURCES

The History of Mexico

http://www.go2mexico.com/article/history/
http://www.mexconnect.com/mex_/history/historyindex.html
http://lanic.utexas.edu/la/Mexico

The Government of Mexico

http://www.odci.gov/cia/publications/factbook/geos/mx.html
http://www.behindthelabel.org
http://www.mexicolaw.com

INDEX

PICTURE CREDITS

CONTRIBUTORS

Roger E. Hernández is the most widely syndicated columnist writing on Hispanic issues in the United States. His weekly column, distributed by King Features, appears in some 40 newspapers across the country, including the *Washington Post*, *Los Angeles Daily News*, *Dallas Morning News*, *Arizona Republic*, *Rocky Mountain News* in Denver, *El Paso Times*, and *Hartford Courant*. He is also the author of *Cubans in America*, an illustrated history of the Cuban presence in what is now the United States, from the early colonists in 16th-century Florida to today's Castro-era exiles. The book was designed to accompany a PBS documentary of the same title.

Hernández's articles and essays have been published in the *New York Times*, *New Jersey Monthly*, *Reader's Digest*, and *Vista Magazine*; he is a frequent guest on television and radio political talk shows, and often travels the country to lecture on his topic of expertise. Currently, he is teaching journalism and English composition at the New Jersey Institute of Technology in Newark, where he holds the position of writer-in-residence. He is also a member of the adjunct faculty at Rutgers University.

Hernández left Cuba with his parents at the age of nine. After living in Spain for a year, the family settled in Union City, New Jersey, where Hernandez grew up. He attended Rutgers University, where he earned a BA in Journalism in 1977; after graduation, he worked in television news before moving to print journalism in 1983. He lives with his wife and two children in Upper Montclair, New Jersey.

Clarissa Aykroyd is a graduate of the University of Victoria in British Colombia, Canada. She has written non-fiction and fiction for journals, newspapers, anthologies, and computer programs. She has also authored books on the exploration of California and on Native American horsemanship for Mason Crest. Her interests include history, Arthurian legend, Sherlock Holmes, and music.

64